PRINCE

of Yesteryear

Part I

Chips Barber

OBELISK PUBLICATIONS

ALSO BY THE AUTHOR
Diary of a Dartmoor Walker
Diary of a Devonshire Walker
The Great Little Dartmoor Book
The Great Little Chagford Book
Made in Devon *(with David FitzGerald)*
Beautiful Dartmoor
Dark and Dastardly Dartmoor *(with Sally Barber)*
Weird and Wonderful Dartmoor *(with Sally Barber)*
Ghastly and Ghostly Devon *(with Sally Barber)*
Haunted Pubs in Devon *(with Sally Barber)*
Ten Family Walks on Dartmoor *(with Sally Barber)*
Tales of the Teign *(with Judy Chard)*
Cranmere Pool – The First Dartmoor Letterbox
Six Short Pub Walks on Dartmoor *(with Sally Barber)*

OTHER BOOKS IN THIS SERIES
Ashburton of Yesteryear, *John Germon and Pete Webb*
The Teign Valley of Yesteryear, *Chips Barber*
Brixham of Yesteryear, *Chips Barber*
Pinhoe of Yesteryear, *Chips Barber*
Princetown of Yesteryear Part II, *Chips Barber*

We have over 100 Devon related titles; for further details please send an SAE to Obelisk Publications at the address below, or telephone (01392) 468556.

**All photos belong to the collection of Rosie Oxenham
Thanks to Mr K. E. Ruth for permission to use pics on page 15**

Rosie Oxenham would like to dedicate this book to the memory of a very dear friend, Gloria

*First published in 1995
by Obelisk Publications, 2 Church Hill, Pinhoe, Exeter, Devon
Designed by Chips and Sally Barber
Typeset by Sally Barber
Printed in Great Britain by
The Devonshire Press Limited, Torquay, Devon*

PRINCETOWN

of Yesteryear

Part I

Princetown sits high up on the roof of Devon, some 1,400 feet above sea level. It is a remote, rainy, windswept place where the mist often envelopes it with its grey mantle. But, despite this damp and dreary image, there are many people who love the splendid isolation, the great open aspect of a small town with a wide main street. Rosie Oxenham is such a person who has, for a great many years, indulged in her passion of collecting old picture postcards and photographs of Princetown. That collection is an impressive and valuable one for it visually records what the town has been like over the last one hundred years. Here, then, is just a selection of the pictures in it.

We start with the railway that once was an important lifeline with the 'outside world'. Princetown had one of the highest railway stations in England at 1,372 feet above sea level. Other notable highly-elevated stations, of the past, included Barras, in Westmorland at 1,100 feet, Troutbeck in Cumberland 949 feet, Alston, also in Cumberland at 930 feet and Ashbury, near Okehampton, at 805 feet.

According to the British Railways' publication, 'Holiday Guide Area No.4,' Princetown was "Approached by a branch railway which climbs the wild hills like a goat …"

Here we have three different views of Princetown's station. In the above view the detached building on the left was the Stationmaster's house. In the middle picture scaffolding can be seen behind the station. This had been erected during the construction of New Station Cottages.

The passenger railway line had a life that spanned from 1883-1956. Anyone who is old enough to remember riding on this branch line will tell you just what a wonderful ride it was up from Yelverton, the line twisting around giant curves as it climbed up the sides of many of Dartmoor's hills and tors to reach Princetown.

The tall tower of St Michael's Church at Princetown is a landmark for miles around. Not a lot has changed, in the above view, but the lamps have gone from atop the granite pillars at the entrance. Many walkers, out on the open moors, have been able to get their bearings from this fine building when their eyesight hasn't been quite keen enough to detect the pencil-thin television mast on North Hessary Tor. The church was largely built by French and American prisoners of war. This is why you will find the French and American flags, along with the Union flag, inside. As some two hundred Americans died whilst at Princetown, a memorial window, on the east side of the church, was given, in 1910, by the 'National Society of the United States Daughters of 1812.' This adds a touch of colour to a town where the grey of granite predominates. There is an inscription on the cemetery wall to the south of the church which states: "In Memory of Three Valiant soldiers of the 7th Royal Fusiliers who died on Dartmoor in a snowdrift, 12th February 1853, Corporal Joseph Panton, aged 20, Private Patrick Carlin, aged 23, George Driver, aged 27." The sad story that lead to this memorial is included with the Devil's Elbow picture on page 29. Perhaps the most appropriate tablet of all is one to Sir Thomas Tyrwhitt "whose name and memory are inseparable from all great works in Dartmoor" or so it is said. He was the man responsible for the prison, Princetown's principal *raison d'être*.

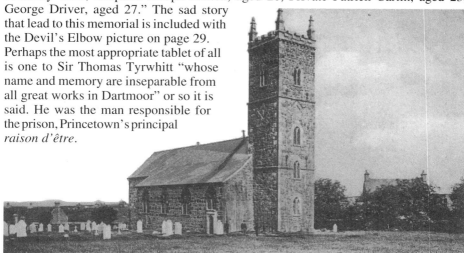

Tyrwhitt's initial late-18th century dream for the area in and around Princetown was to turn the upland barren wastes of Dartmoor into productive farmland. Although he had a small degree of success, the elevation and its resultant harsh climate eventually won the day and his great scheme was all but abandoned. However, in the early part of the 19th century the various conflicts with France, and then America, led to a situation where many prisoners of war had been captured but there was a lack of space in which to hold them. There was particular concern over thousands of Frenchmen held in hulks at Plymouth. Tyrwhitt had the answer, a War Depot at Princetown. Although the history is well documented, there are only a few visible reminders of that time when many thousands of men were held, from 24 May 1809, in extremely tough conditions. The last prisoners left in January 1816. In between the death toll reached almost 1,500! Above is the arch leading to the American Prisoners of War cemetery, Americans accounting for more than two hundred of the total who died in Princetown. The obelisk below is one of two such memorials to the dead, one for the Americans and the other for the French.

On this page and overleaf are some aerial views from yesteryear, of Princetown and its prison. The prison was born out of necessity as will be seen. The War Depot, of Tyrwhitt's time, following the repatriation and subsequent departure of all the prisoners of war, became derelict whilst Princetown resembled a ghost town. There was little or nothing to sustain the town so it returned, once more, to a quiet settlement. The main activities in the area, throughout the 1830s and 40s, were the extensive granite quarries not far from the town.

The years passed by, Britain coping with its criminals in the time-honoured tradition of piling those who committed minor misdeeds into overcrowded urban prisons, transporting those deemed guilty of slightly more serious offences to the other side of the world and stringing up those perpetrators of the most serious offences. But the times, they were a-

changing and the various colonies, one by one, were starting to lay the law down themselves about accepting our criminals. By the mid 19th century there was nowhere to send them and the penal system cried out for a place of detention on mainland Britain so once again Princetown was back in business!

In the intervening years the prison has had a colourful past and has become such a feature of the moor that if the word 'Dartmoor' is mentioned in other parts of this country, the chances are high that the mental image formed is that of the prison. There are those who will recall some of the escapes, who will remember some of the dubious characters 'banged up' here and will have this notion of men, complete with ball and chain, slaving away breaking rocks in the granite quarry near the prison. Today, although it's far from being a holiday camp, as some have wrongly tagged it, it's a less severe regime than in the days of old.

Anyone who has ever done the Abbots' Way walk will probably recognise this view, having strolled past South Hessary Tor towards Princetown. This is the scene ahead as a lunch time stop beckons. It's amazing to see how the spirits of walkers are lifted on this downward slope. The prison can be seen in the top right of the picture and the church is seen towards the top left.

Below a trail of steam wafts behind a locomotive on the railway line between Princetown and Yelverton. Here the train is passing King's Tor, not far from Princetown, on its slow journey along this scenic line. Had it survived it would have provided one of the best railway rides in England.

Here we have two pictures, of the past, taken whilst looking in opposite directions. They are both taken in those days when horse-drawn modes of transport were the norm, the end result being a much quieter scene, traffic-wise, than is the case these days. The top picture is taken outside Bolt's Stores which is on the left hand side of the picture. The Bolt brothers can be seen by their cart, a little way along the road in the direction of Two Bridges. An interested onlooker is sat on the window sill of the tea rooms on the right. This was also Bowden's Guest House, one of many places where people could stay in Princetown.

Below the view is looking up Plymouth Hill and a number of young ladies have shown that they are not camera shy. On the far left is a drinking trough, a welcome sight to leg-weary travellers and footsore animals.

The two pictures on this page are from the age of the motor car and both show vehicles outside the Duchy Hotel. Moorland ponies have wandered into town in search of scraps of food from visitors. This they could only do until about 1965 when cattle grids were placed on the edge of town to stop the pony invasion. The building at the back left of the top picture was Ivy House. To the right of it is the Plume of Feathers, one of Princetown's most famous buildings. It was built in 1785 and one of its earliest functions was to accommodate the work force that had been engaged to build Tor Royal for Thomas Tyrwhitt. Cars can no longer park on the spot where they are shown here as the area has been paved to set off the former Duchy Hotel, just visible on the right hand edge of the top picture. This has become the High Dartmoor Interpretation Centre, housed in a building whose history is inextricably entwined with that of Princetown's. Today it a centre which informs and educates people about Dartmoor, using a range of modern techniques to show the moor's heritage, uses and management.

The Duchy Hotel has entertained many famous guests and there is good reason for 'Sherlock Holmes' to be stood at the bottom of the staircase today, with a cardboard cutout of Arthur Conan Doyle peering over his shoulder. The latter stayed here when this was the Duchy Hotel. Driven here by horse and coach with a driver called Baskerville, Conan Doyle used his imagination, no doubt inspired by his own wanderings over the moor, to create his famous book, "The Hound of the Baskervilles" in 1902. Foxtor Mires, about three miles to the south of Princetown, became the Grimpen Mire of the book. It's widely believed that at least part of this book was written whilst staying here. The Duchy Hotel was built in 1785 and in over two centuries it has undergone numerous changes, some of which can be seen in the pictures on these pages. However, none of them will be old enough to show an old toll gate that stood outside the hotel until about 1854. This was Barrack Gate and was one of two at either end of the road that ran from Rundlestone to this point. The gate served as a boundary mark to show the extent of the lands under the jurisdiction of the prison. Part of it was taken to Brimpts, near Dartmeet, where it was used as an entrance gate. Recycling is obviously not a new concept!

Above is view of the inside of the Duchy Hotel looking as smart as its advert seemed to suggest that it was.

Below is a special occasion, not only in the former hotel's history but also in Princetown's as a Royal visit is in progress. The orderly crowd has been kept well back from the hotel's entrance as the Royal party has just arrived. The Prince and Princess of Wales, no strangers to Devon, made this visit in 1909. The following year the Prince of Wales became George V ruling until his death in 1936.

Adverts, in early guide books, reveal that Aaron Rowe owned the Duchy Hotel in the early part of the twentieth century, the highest hostelry in the land, but it tells us nothing of the man, a pillar of the church, who lived at the time when the celebrated Dartmoor explorer and writer, William Crossing, was planning his "Guide to Dartmoor". William Crossing asked Aaron if he knew anyone capable of doing some topographical sketches for his intended book. Dame Fortune was smiling on Crossing for Aaron knew just the right man, a young chap called Philip Guy Stevens, who was courting his daughter. Philip was a clerk at the prison, had a good locational knowledge of the moor and was blessed with the cartographical skills to create sketch maps of it. Once he had been introduced to Crossing he followed the master moorman's instructions to go hither and thither across moor and mire, over bog and bracken in the wet and wind or in the heat and haze to compile a portfolio of sketches that would later bring the all-embracing guide to life.

There were several worded versions of advertisements placed in brochures and guide books – one is shown in *Princetown of Yesteryear Part II* – another states that it's "the highest hostelry in the Land" and adds that it's "Situated amid the finest of the Tors, with charming and varied scenery. Within easy reach of Villages, Menhirs, Stone Crosses, &c. Excellent Salmon and Trout Fishing. Good Hunting. Open and closed Carriages. Home Dairy." On the floor of the entrance visitors were greeted by the words of a mosaic set in the floor that greeted them with "Welcome the coming". The pure genius continued for when the guests departed the mosaic read "Speed the parting guest". Aaron Rowe was a genial host who ran a fine homely hotel in a town that can be a stark one at times, in the Pre-Gortex Age, when the mists envelop the hills or when the wind whistles through it with a malevolent intent.

Below is a picture of Bolt's Store and house, opposite the Duchy Hotel, as it looked in 1904.

Most of the pictures presented in this book were, originally, postcards sent by both locals and holidaymakers. These two pictures show two Princetown Post Offices of the past but from different times. This is where most of those cards were probably posted and over the years a mountain of messages would have passed through these establishments, what a story they could tell! Above is the first post office where the library is now located and below is the second post office. To confuse matters the third is on the opposite side of the street, where the Imperial Hotel was and then, about 1981, moved back to site number two, where it still is today.

Above is an old view of Lords Cafe in Princetown a catering business whose name has been associated with Princetown for many generations. The name is still in existence but the personnel and premises have changed as Lloyds Bank now occupy the site. The gap next to Lloyds is now a flat roofed extension to the Dartmoor Gift Shop. Below a procession is in progress to celebrate the Coronation Day of King George V who was crowned on 19 June 1911. It was noticeable that the great width of Princetown's main street was a problem for those whose job it was to hang out the bunting and, no doubt, they kept their fingers crossed that the day wouldn't be too windy.

The obvious place to erect a war memorial to the dead of the First World War was the open space of the village green, the perfect place to set off the commemorative cross. Here we see its opening ceremony, which was a poignant ceremony for those who gathered there all knew of young persons who had been killed in this conflict.

Below is a later scene showing the wider view with the war memorial, just left of centre. The picture also includes the former Imperial Hotel, at the time being used as Princetown Post Office, on the left side of the picture.

Princetown looks anything but a tourist mecca in these two views from the early twentieth century, a far cry from how it is depicted a few years later. A Dartmoor guide book from the 1928-29 season had this to say of Princetown. *Princetown differs from other centres in being right on the Moor. Little more than a village, it has come to its own as 'the highest town in England,' and has won repute for the rare and health-giving qualities of its air. It offers every convenience and comfort in the way of hotel and other accommodation, while the railway keeps it in touch with the outer world, and motor buses connect it directly with Tavistock. In the holiday season motor-coaches from all over the West Country converge on it, and during luncheon time its square can hardly find room for all the vehicles of various sizes, colours and names that park there. The restaurants are filled to overflowing while people who prefer an alfresco meal dot the neighbouring slopes.* These pictures were obviously taken on a very different sort of a Princetown day.

A Dartmoor guide book for 1929 lists Princetown's three hotels as being the Duchy, the Imperial and the Prince of Wales. The tariffs are only stated for the Imperial. A single room and board was six shillings and sixpence whilst a double was, surprisingly, double the amount! Lunch was two shillings and sixpence, afternoon tea a shilling and dinner three shillings. The tariffs compared favourably with most other Dartmoor hotels, the Imperial's being appreciably cheaper than the Two Bridges Hotel. Although these two pictures of the Imperial are similar there are differences. A loft or two, perhaps a porch, a bit of rendering or other changes have taken place between the shoots. If you haven't worked it out yet, the one above is the more recent for there are no rooms shown in the post office roof on the left side of the picture as pictured below. The Imperial Hotel no longer exists and about the only place, in Princetown proper, that accommodates appreciable, if that's an appropriate word, numbers of long-stay guests, these days, is the one with a massive wall all around its perimeter!

Above is the one place where you wouldn't have purchased this book even though it was a branch of that famous booksellers W.H. Smith & Son. Here the small shack-like building on the left was their Princetown branch. The company that rose to fame from its station bookstalls must have realised that this was not a sufficiently commercial proposition as the nearest branch is now some seven miles away at Tavistock. Next door, farther along Tavistock Road, was the Princetown and District Co-op shop. This was a business, thriving at one time, that had its foundation stone laid on 14 July 1894. In its last years it gave sterling service as Princetown's youth club. However, these businesses and their premises have both been demolished, the latter in 1989.

Below, and still farther along the road towards the prison, is another scene to have witnessed considerable change. On the left are New Villas and opposite them are the long-since departed buildings of Government Row, which were originally known as Church Row on account of their proximity to the church, along the road and on the right side of this view.

The picture above shows the imposing dwellings known as Devonshire Flats. These were located opposite the church but became in a such a state that they were demolished. However on the back of the card was this message, which lives on nearly a century after it was scribbled. 'Josie' was chuffed to bits on 2 May 1907 when she sent this card off to her friend, Mrs Marks of Parkhurst on the IOW, for she wrote of great elation at passing her exam.

Below is the clearly recognisable Hessary Terrace.

Rain stop play? Can you imagine how many rain affected matches or ones interrupted by bad light there must be in a place with so much precipitation? This one though shows a match in progress between the prison officers and the staff of Plymouth School – in 1906. The message on the back relates these details and goes on to say that the next card will be one showing the players who took part in the match. It was common for photographers to print up postcards of such things as this, perhaps even scenes that we wouldn't consider as worthy these days. However their dedication has proved to be a real legacy as people and places, now long gone, are only recorded in pictures of this type. The picture below shows the participants from another game, this time between 'Married' and 'Single' men. Hope the little lad in the front was playing for the 'Single' men!

The next sequence of pictures takes us out into that glorious countryside that is Princetown's back garden. We first head along the road to Two Bridges where the West Dart River flows ever onwards towards its confluence with the East Dart River at Dartmeet several miles downstream. The hotel is well placed for those who love Dartmoor, in all its moods, at a meeting place of roads. In the picture above, looking from the Princetown side of the river, a road junction can be seen at the top right. The road to the right is the one that eventually, after many twists and turns and ups and downs, reaches Ashburton on the edge of the moor. The way to the left is the road on to Postbridge and beyond. The hotel was originally called the Saracen's Head and remained so until 1893. It is an eighteenth century building that has had its share of past problems, most notable incident being a serious fire in 1866 that threatened to completely destroy it, only the outer walls standing, somewhat unsafely afterwards.

Above is a view taken from Rundlestone Tor looking over the top of the small hamlet of Rundlestone towards the towering mass of Great Mistor. Below is the legendary Devil's Elbow, a bend about half a mile to the south west of Princetown, scene of a great tragedy. It was February 1853 when the 7th Regiment of Royal Fusiliers were doing their tour of garrison duty at Princetown. The sub-zero conditions and the sea of white snow that had formed into great waves of drifts had polarised much of the activity. Nevertheless Corporal Joseph Panton reported for duty. Despite the blizzard his orders were to walk to Dousland and then escort two replacement troops back to Princetown. The walk was arduous and the going was treacherous – it took young Panton four hours to complete. He was accompanied by another man called Smith who urged him not to attempt the return journey. Despite the advice the 20 year-old, newly married corporal followed his orders. He met the two privates – Patrick Carlin and George Driver – at the inn and when they had rested from their own march up from St George's Barracks in Devonport, they set out for Princetown. They were never seen alive again. The two young privates made it as far as the Devil's Elbow shown below. Corporal Panton's body was found just two hundred yards from the back of the Duchy Hotel.

Merrivale, straddling the River Walkham, a few miles along the road to Tavistock, was much more of a community in the past. Then there were far more people living and working in the district, the quarries working full tilt to produce blocks of granite for a variety of uses. The upright picture (opposite) shows a row of terraced dwellings, known as Merrivale Cottages, where about a dozen workers and their families lived. These cottages were demolished many years ago. Eden Philpotts, a great Dartmoor writer, took the Dartmoor Inn at Merrivale and translated it into the Jolly Huntsman for his colourful novel "The Mother." In it a memorable wedding breakfast is enjoyed at the inn whilst all the major action of the book centres on the nearby King's Tor area, high on the hills to the south east of Merrivale. These pictures of yesteryear also show the main Tavistock–Princetown road as a much narrower thoroughfare than the present one. There are now two bridges at Merrivale and the pub, which was originally much smaller, uses part of the old road as a car park for its patrons. An examination of the picture here

shows the cottages in descending height. About 1920 they were incorporated into the pub and their height was increased to give the more uniform appearance of today's pub. As most of the dividing walls of this former line of cottages have been removed, it's hard to appreciate what they must have been like when they were first built in the seventeenth century.

The date on the back of one of the cards posted at Princetown was dated 17 July 1929. It was sent to the Rev. Dom Swithun Bell OSB at St Mary's in Leyland Lancashire. The sender had been to Buckfast Abbey the previous day and had not found the experience too uplifting for he complained of "...a seething mass [presumably no pun intended] of charabanc trippers in the church taken around in lots of about a 100 by monastic guides! A nightmare! Never again!" The picture below conveys what those vehicles were like, the drivers attired to combat the rigours of moorland weather, the passengers bracing themselves for a similar encounter with the elements.

We finish with two views of Dartmoor's oldest and largest reservoir, that of Burrator. The above one is taken near Burrator Halt on the railway to Princetown. The viaduct, across the reservoir, was constructed in 1926 to maintain access to those who lived on the Sheepstor village side of the Meavy valley whilst the dam's height was added to in order to increase the capacity of the lake behind it.

We hope that you have enjoyed this nostalgic look back at a "Princetown of Yesteryear" as seen through just a small selection of the marvellous pictures that Rosie Oxenham has collected through the years. If it's true when they say that a good picture is worth a thousand words then this is, indeed, a much larger book than it might appear at first glance!